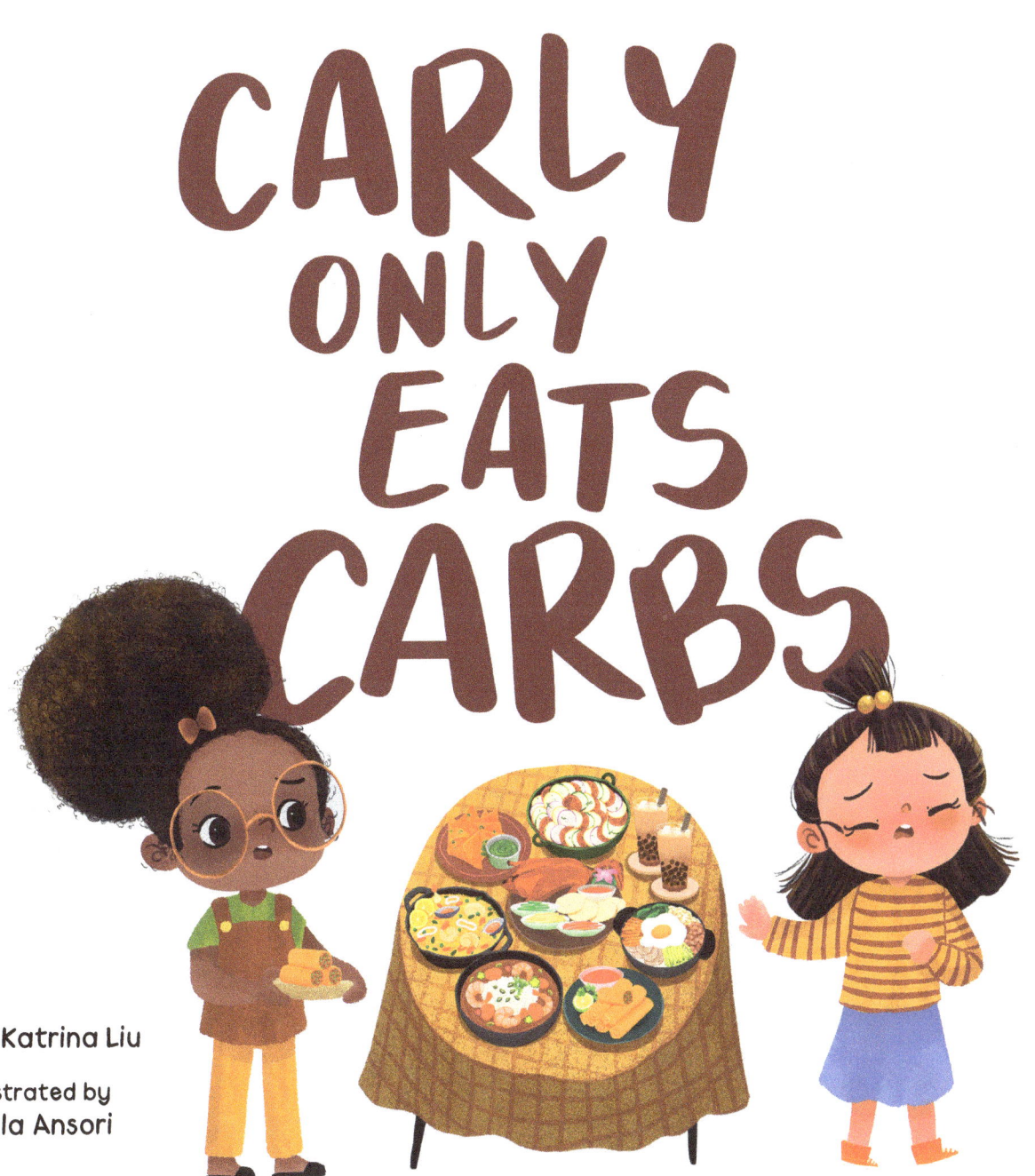

CARLY ONLY EATS CARBS

by Katrina Liu

Illustrated by Bella Ansori

This is Carly. Carly never backed down from a new adventure.

She's tried skiing, snorkeling and even rock climbing!

She especially loved adventures with her best friend, Olivia.

In fact, the only thing Carly wasn't adventurous with was food.

Carly was what her parents called a "very picky eater."

Carly only ate from a short list: bread, rice, buttered noodles... As long as it was a carb, she was happy to gobble it up!

French fries were her absolute favorite. Carly could eat them every day if she'd had her way!

"Why don't you try some eggs?" Mom asked at breakfast.
"Or some bacon?" Dad offered.

Carly refused. She'd stick with pancakes and the occasional waffle.

At lunchtime, her friends often shared foods so they could try new things.

"Have some grapes!" Olivia said.

"Would you like to try some sushi?" another asked.

Carly shook her head. Then she ate the bread from her sandwich and tossed the rest in the trash.

At dinner, Carly's parents prepared baked chicken and broccoli. "They're good!" Mom said.

"Just try!" said Dad.

Carly took her plate. Then, when no one was watching, she secretly fed her meal to her dog, Bun-bun.

It was the day of Olivia's birthday sleepover party.
Carly arrived in her new french fry pajamas.

Olivia greeted her with a big hug.
"Wait until you see what we've set up!"

"It's my around-the-world party! We've got games and music from all over the world. Best of all, we have yummy foods from many different countries!" Olivia said with excitement.

"Isn't it amazing?!" said Olivia.

Carly's eyes widened at a table filled with so many strange and colorful foods.

"Do you have anything less colorful?
Like buttered noodles or french fries?"
Carly asked.

Olivia's face fell. "I'm sorry.
We don't have any of those things."

"That's okay!" Carly said, trying to smile.
"I'll just wait for the birthday cake."

"Oh. Actually, we're not having birthday cake,"
Olivia informed. "We're having Japanese
mochi with sweet red bean for dessert."

Carly's smile dropped. There was nothing here for her to eat, and it was a sleepover. That meant she would go hungry all night!

Everyone at the party danced and played games. Carly tried to join in, but the more she ran around, the more her stomach began to rumble.

"Dinner!"
Olivia's mom announced.

Sounds of "Yum!" and "Mmmm!" filled the room.

Olivia noticed Carly with an empty plate. "Just think of it as one of our adventures together!" Olivia told her encouragingly.

Carly did enjoy going on adventures with Olivia. And of course, she loved her best friend. She didn't want her to feel bad, especially not on her birthday.

"Try it, Carly! You can do it!" her friends cheered.

Hesitantly, Carly took a tiny spoonful of seafood paella and started to chew.

Amazing flavors and textures danced around in her mouth.
"Mmmmmm!" she exclaimed, spooning in another bite.

Carly began to take bites of the other foods. Every dish had a wonderful and unique flavor, like nothing she'd ever tasted!

"WOW! I never knew foods could taste this good! Why didn't anyone tell me to try them?" she asked.

Everyone burst into laughter. "Oh, Carly!" Olivia giggled. "You really are one of a kind!"

For Mina & Leah,
The inspiration for everything I do.

About the Author

Katrina Liu is an American-born Chinese mom and indie author living in San Francisco, California. Her daughters inspired her to create books where they can see themselves reflected in the characters. She hopes to add more Asian representation into the world of children's books. Katrina has written and published several titles that feature Asian-American characters and culture. She also has many bilingual books available in Chinese and English for non-native speakers.

ISBN 978-1-953281-75-3

Copyright © 2022 by Katrina Liu. All rights reserved. No part of this book may be reproduced, transmitted, or stored in an information retrieval system in any form or by any means, graphic, electronic, or mechanical, including photocopying, taping, and recording, without prior written permission from the publisher. First edition 2022. Also available in a bilingual Chinese editions.

Other popular titles by Katrina Liu

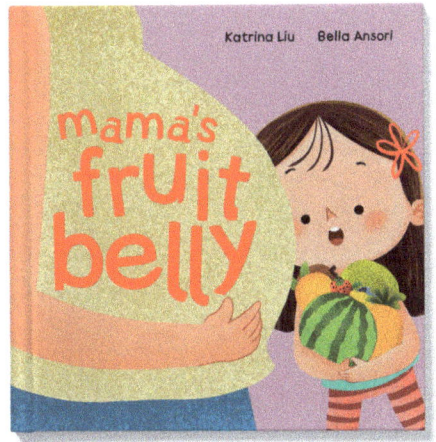

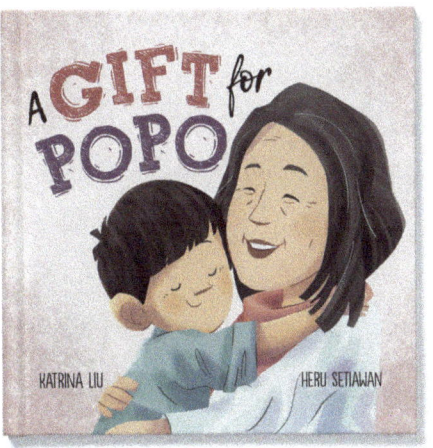
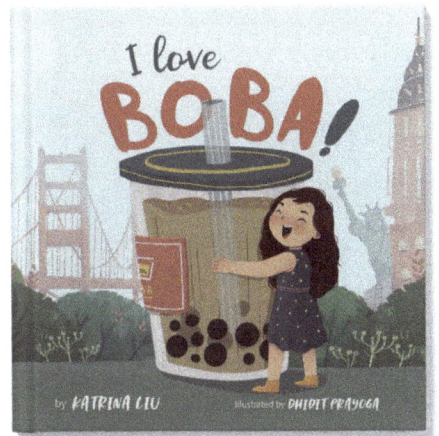

For more books by Katrina Liu visit
www.lycheepress.com

CPSIA information can be obtained
at www.ICGtesting.com
Printed in the USA
LVHW071006291122
734247LV00005B/24